FALLING APART

ARSH

dedicated to every person who read this book...

you're heard, you're seen, you're felt.

Contents

Contents

Acknowledgements

I'd like to thank Abhishek Arora, the first person to tell me that I should publish my poems. I'd like to thank Sahil Multani, for constantly helping and encouraing me through the entire publishing process. To Niyati Panchal, Heet Shah and Sahil, a heartfelt gratitude for being there as I wrote my poems and prepared myself to publish them. This wouldn't have been possible without you guys.

1. Goodbye

Why can't we ever truly say goodbye?
even when we say goodbye,
we keep coming back.
One day, one week, one month later,
we find ourselves at the same crossroads
we first met at, near the desert shop.
The close sign blinking in different colours,
the street lamp always flickering.
The same black eyes, looking at each other,
the same hands, itching for a touch.
A half smoked cigarette in my hand,
a half-drunk wine bottle in yours.
With a light chuckle, we walk together
to the beach wall, putting our things down,
we face each other, our eyes meeting once again,
I take a small step forward,
you take another step towards me.
We meet mid-way, and embrace each other.
Standing on my toes, fitting in your neck and shoulder,
we hold each other tightly,
trying to fill the void that we've felt.
Reluctantly, you break the embrace,
and we sit on the wall.
A bottle of wine in one hand,
a cigarette in the other.

And two hands, holding each other.
Filling the spaces between our fingers.

•2•

2. Pain

She held in a shudder,
so as to not make any noise.
Exhaling through her mouth,
eyes slowly closing,
tears gently falling.
She bit her lip hard,
making blood come out.
Shivering into the cold night,
sitting on the porch,
knees to her chest and
hands tucked in front of the stomach.
She wanted to scream, cry out loud
but she couldn't, which only
made the tears fall faster and longer.
How do you emote without anyone not seeing?
How do you express without being judged for it?
How do you cry out in pain without
having to answer the source of your pain?
You don't.
You simply cannot.
Because, even in pain,
You cannot have it all.

3. Sunrise

He felt like a sunrise on a cold winter morning,
Like waking up around warm cozy blankets.
Feeling his warm breath on my cold cheeks,
Like warm summer breeze.
His warm fingers finding their way to my cold ones,
Intertwining them together, no space in between.
Our feet, playing hide and seek.

He felt like a sunrise on a cold winter morning,
Warm lips gently kissing my shoulder,
Slowly making their way to my cheeks.
His eyes piercing into mine, oozing love,
The sun rays softly falling on us from the curtains;
Lighting up his honey brown eyes,
Giving fireworks in my heart.

4. Blossom

Tired of the chaos in her mind,
she turned around to run from life.
A midst the turn, she heard a meek voice
'stop, don't go.' the voice proposed.
She turned around to look for the voice,
instead found herself staring at an image.
An image, exactly like hers.
Dressed in the same attire and accessories,
she realized it was she who stopped her,
taking a step forward, she raised her hand;
gently touching the surface of the mirror.
She sighed, 'who are you?', in reply
her voice echoed.
Bewildered, she looked closely at the image staring back at her,
she found tiny stars sparkling in the eyes of the image,
cheeks pulled upward in the biggest smile.
skin glowing like an afternoon in spring,
face oozing happiness.
Taking all the in, she felt her heart tug at her,
as if pulling her out of something deep and dark.
She slowly blinked her eyes,
as if it were all a dream, which it wasn't.
She focused on the image and found it staring back,
Realizing that it's her inner self, it's her hope.
Hope, that's things will be okay.

Hope, that the pieces of her puzzle with fit into places.
She stopped, sighed and then smiled.
Because her inner self had finally blossomed.

5. Void

I've felt it before, you know.
This nagging hollow feeling in my body.
It's been here before,
she has stayed here before.
We are at that stage where we are well acquainted with each other,
she comes, I welcome it.
she stays for a while, I work through it,
then she leaves and I let her.
Sometimes she even brings gifts for me,
past memories, horrifying thoughts
sad songs and haunting images.
At times, these things are so intense
that I forget how to function properly,
I don't think she realizes the effect she has on me,
but then there are times when I am sure that she's playing games with
me, intentionally.
So, I don't know, if she knows or not.
The thing is, this time when she came,
with that empty feeling, turning my insides out
it didn't feel the same. I think,
I think it was stronger than before,
more intense, more...vehement.
I still welcomed her, of course.
The first few days were okay, normal.
I couldn't feel anything because she made me numb,

I enjoyed that feeling.
Suddenly, things became gray,
I couldn't separate black and white,
I was drowning in gray. Funny,
for she was the one who taught me how to swim.
I tried catching my breath,
to reach the surface just once, but I couldn't.
She had taken me so deep this time,
I lost my way, I let her take control.
And so, here I was falling slowly;
in my own pool of tears and blood,
hurtful words coming back,
memories of the past resurfacing,
thoughts running wild like it's a race course.
My body physically refusing to move,
mentally, I don't even know if I was there,
conscious about what was happening.
spiritually, I could feel myself leave my body.
starting from my legs,
slowly creeping to my head.
I think the worst part was, that
I didn't want to stop it.
I was okay with it.
I was laying there;
shivering and numb,
letting her take me away,
away from this world.
Away from this nuisance,
away from this life.

6. Fear

I haven't been able to write anything,
and it's eating me up.
There's too much I've kept in.
But I'm at a loss of words to rant it out.
All that's left now is tears. But even they seem to leaving now.
That's what happens, doesn't it?
I attach myself to someone,
and then they leave.
It's not like I asked to feel so much,
I was okay being the numb aloof kid.
I had gotten used to it. Until,
I saw you the other day. And my world,
turned upside down.
Now there are too many feelings,
feelings I can't seem to control.
There are too many thoughts
running wild in my mind like it's a race.
There are too many memories,
that is rather just forget.
But who am I kidding here?
We don't always get what we want.
We can't always control who we fall for.
I wish we could though.
It would be nice to know someone inside out before deciding to fall
for them.

It would be nice to be in control on my feelings and thoughts for
once.
It would be nice to just slow down.
Be in a moment, take it all in properly.
Until you're ready in your mind and soul.
Until you've overcome that fear in your spirit.

7. Transcend

Come dance with me
Like the clouds.
Slow, elegant, with the wind;
Let's make the sky our dance floor,
Changing colors with our mood,
Giving emotions to our moves.
The soft, passionate and
Never ending sky,
Taking us to a place,
So pure and magical;
All the while, us
Being rooted at the same spot.

8. Sad Playlist

Why don't we just make a sad playlist?
With back to back sad songs?
An endless loop of sadness.
Each song makes you cry;
where at every word you are hurt,
after every sentence there's regrets;
And at the end of every paragraph,
You can't help but let out a sigh.
They say love is the strongest feeling,
I say they're wrong.
Sadness is the strongest feeling.
Love makes us do crazy things, yes
But it's the sadness that leads to crime and poetry
I have seen authors hitting inspiration after drag of smoke or a cup of
caffeine,
I have seen poets drunk and drowning in sadness spilling words of
wisdom.
It is always sadness for me;
That makes me go in search of pen and paper,
Or any surface to let everything out.
Let's make a sad playlist, the one
which makes us cry, the one
which pulls words from our my mind's.
The world needs literature to rely on,
But me, oh! darling,

I need sadness to rely on.

Every song is an arrow to your heart if you're in sorrow.

Otherwise it's just mere words set into beats,

I always begin with swollen eyelids,

and shaky lips, my vision going blurry

because of unsettled tears.

But by the end,

A soft exhale leaves my mouth,

Eyelids blinking slowly, my thoughts

a little clear than before.

My mind more peaceful, like

It's ready for another sad playlist.

9. Sunrise

There is nothing more beautiful,
then watching the sun rise.
The clouds sitting on the sky,
like balls of cotton fluffs.
The sun playing hide and seek in between them
The sky adorned with colors of the sun,
crimson over the greyish blue.
The orange hue tainting the white clouds,
Almost as if it were the sun kissing the clouds.
The birds chirping in the back,
Like an ode from them to the sky,
The sunlight slowly creeping up on everything in the world
Giving them colors of happy;
It felt mesmerizing, truly!
Watching the sky change colors
From the beautiful dark midnight blue,
To a slightly brighter sea Blue,
With hints of purple and magenta,
Leaning towards an amber hue,
Golden peeking from the clouds,
Like orange candy in the sky,
Mixing with the now bright blue sky.
If you look closely, you'll notice the dull clouds
Blending in the bright ones.
Hiding from the sky in a coy manner.

It sounds very familiar, doesn't it?
You can feel the sunlight slowly
Touching your tanned skin,
Making you feel like an orange fireball,
Ready to hit the world!
Isn't it amazing? How many feelings
A simple yet beautiful sunrise can make you feel!

10. Waves

It was getting a little dark,
But neither of us wanted to move.
We just kept staring ahead of us,
Listening to the waves thrust.
I think, we were a little scared,
That we would be the wrong pair.
The air around us was humid,
And our bodies were a little timid.
So, we just sat there,
Soaking every bit of it.
In all our glory bare,
Our minds about to admit.
The waves came and went,
The mat flew and settled.
Our clothes linger with each other's scent.
While our hearts still battled.

11. Losing

I don't remember what we talked about,
But I do remember that day.
It was around 6 in the evening,
And you had promised me a cup of chai.
We were sitting on the terrace wall,
Our feet dangling in opposite directions,
Mine on the side, and yours outside.
The air was humid, and there was heaviness in the air,
Until the breeze slowly started flowing,
Into your hair, making it dance,
To my still wet from the wash hair.
The sky was a dull orange as the sun was setting,
And our usual banter resounding through the air.
We watched the sun go down and the sky
Turn to a dark blue with the clouds adorning it.
Our empty cups kept in between,
Like a line which we never crossed.
You were on your side, as I was on mine.
But there was something in the wind that night,
That left me feeling naked with a sense of loss.

12. Shine

It was still dark outside
when my eyes suddenly opened.
Hair sticking to my face,
a sheen of sweat on my body.
The bed sheets crumpled underneath me,
the night blank dimly lit.
Oreo meowed softly at me,
as if saying, 'go back to sleep.'
But instead, I got up from the bed,
tied my hair in a high ponytail,
I stripped out of my damp clothes
and stepped under the shower.
I let the cold water wash away this sickly feeling,
leaving goosebumps on my warm skin.
I wore a fresh pair of clothes,
put my shoes on and trudged down.
Oreo was still sound asleep,
without a care of the chaos.
I walked outside the door and then the gate,
feeling the cold air on my body.
I inhaled the crisp air,
savoring this moment for a second
and then started walking, to no where.
My feet crunching the gravel, as I walk
the birds yet to wake with their call.

As I walked under the light from moon,

There was nothing but darkness around,

except for a few porch lights,

accidentally left on.

I don't know for how long was I walking,

or what exactly my destination was,

but I found myself standing by the canal bridge,

the soft sound of the river flowing beneath,

the wind whooshing gently, the trees swaying lightly.

I slowly looked up to see the moon had set,

and the sun was about to rise,

the birds were up and about, chirping their way around.

I stood there for about 18 minutes,

Just staring at the scene in front of me.

The river temptingly flowing,

The trees gushingly swaying,

The birds cheerfully chirping,

The sun godly shining.

13. Love Letter

It was one am and the light was still on,
Faint classical music playing in the back.
You walked into the room,
In all your tired yet handsome glory,
Two mugs in hand, one of coffee and one of tea.
I was sitting at the desk, typing away on the laptop.
An already empty cup on my desk,
Which you replaced with a new full one.
You bent down and hugged me from behind,
A lingering kiss at the side of my head.
I leaned into you, slowly inhaling your vanilla scent.
Our room dimly lit with the blue lights
And my bright desk light. You let go of me,
Making me feel the cold air suddenly.
You walked to the corner near the bookshelf
And sat on the bean bag,
Oreo immediately jumping into your lap,
Making himself comfortable there.
You picked up the book, and started reading where you left,
A thousand love letters by famous people.
In the words of Frida Kahlo, you read out loud
"I ask you for violence, in the nonsense,
And you, you give me grace,
Your light and your warmth.
I'd like to paint you, but

There are no colors, because
There are so many, in my confusion,
The tangible form of my great love."
I let out a sigh, and stretched my neck.
You closed the book and removed your glasses.
There was a moment of silence between us,
No movement, no breathing, just pure bliss.
I slowly looked back at you,
And you raised your eyes to me,
We stared at each other in the dimly lit room,
You gave me a small smile and I couldn't help but chuckle.
I closed my laptop and turned off the desk light,
Walked over to you and sat besides you.
I hugged you and comfortably settled myself around you,
You embraced me and let out a sigh of relief.
And we fell asleep to the sound Beethoven in a blue room.
Content. Peaceful. Loved.
That was our love letter to each other.

14. Sun

I have always found comfort in watching the movements of the sun,
Be it an orange gold sunrise or
A pink purple sunset.
There's something about watching the sky
Change colors with the sun slowly.
From dark midnight blue,
To a dull greyish blue,
Beginning with a bright white in the sky,
And going from thousands of shades of orange,
Giving life and colour to every single atom
That comes in its way, going high up,
To becoming the biggest, the most beautiful ball of fire
Is adorning the vivid blue sky.
Watching the bright blue sky of the evening,
Slowly leave the life inside it and turn dark.
At times, with hints of mauve and fuchsia
Or tangerine and red. It feels endless.
It leaves with a calming sense,
A sense of comfort, a sense of knowing.
No matter what, it's always going to be a new day.
There's always going to be another beautiful sunrise.
There's always going to be another breathtaking sunset.
And there's always going to be a chance for you.

15. Moon Child

She tossed and turned,
Not being able to sleep.
Restless thoughts and overwhelming feelings,
Playing games with her again.
Her eyes forcefully shut,
Hoping for a hint of sleep.
But to her dismay, sleep
didn't want to come to her.
She slowly opened her eyes,
Looking through the window, and
saw it, the Moon is all his breathtaking glow.
A dull pale white gray colour,
with black craters adorning him surface.
His light finding it's way into her room,
Gently falling onto her pillow,
so as to not cause her more distress.
The more she stared at him,
The more she felt like he was saying something,
Like he was trying to talk to her.
And maybe he was, after all,
He did have sense of tranquility about him.
Despite all her feeling and thoughts,
that night, she slept a peaceful sleep,
Only to be woken up by the same nightmare.
But this time, she was a little less worried

because, she knew that the moon would be there,
Shining on her, taking care of her, protecting her.

16. Escape

She ran as fast as she could,
Her shoes hitting the pavement,
Hard and in a steady rhythm.
She took a turn on the street her house was on,
A staggered sigh of relief at that sight.
She bit her lips, holding back the tears,
Pushing herself and taking more than she can,
Her body was giving up, she could feel it in her legs.
'Few more meters she thought and kept running,
As soon as she entered the house and,
closed the door, her body gave in.
She fell to the floor, her back against the door.
She just sat there, legs numb,
Face dripping of sweat, hair sticking to her neck,
Chest puffing with short breaths,
Eyes unable to stay open.
This was it, she had done it.
She had gone too far for her body to cope.
But...but why did she feel like this wasn't enough?
Why were the words still ringing in her ears?
Why did she still have the prickly sensation on her hand?
Why did she still feel like she needed to get away?
Escape from the things in the past?
Escape from the things of the present?
And escape to the things in the future?

17. Letting Go

It was a cold winter evening,
and as I stepped out the door,
my warm body shivered a little.
I stepped down the porch and
slowly sat down on the step.
The ground freezing against my bare feet,
I look to the side at all the leaves,
small drops of dew adorning them,
making them heavy and droopy.
I continued to watch the leaves,
the longer I watched,
the more difficult it got to pull away.
My pale skin flushed and my hair
tied on top of my head.
I wrapped my sweater a little tighter,
breathing its smell in.
As I kept my eyes on the leaf,
I saw the dew drops glide and
collect at the tip of the leaf,
making it droop more.
Within a blink of an eye,
the water collected at the tip
fell to the ground. One big drop of water.
My eyes moved to the fallen drop of water,
And my mind re-winded what happened.

One single drop of water, that's all it took.
Just one more drop of water towards the tip,
made the leaf so heavy that it had to let go.
And the second it let go of all the water,
It became a little lighter, stood a little taller.
You are the leaf.
Your past is the dew drop.
Let go. Let it all fall down.
The more we hold onto it,
The more heavy we become.
The more we tend to droop to the ground.
But the minute you decide to let go,
You will become light,
You will stand tall,
Free of all the burden.

18. Memory

Often times when I sit down tired, confused,
with no destination to move forward to,
I fold my hands and lay my head down on them,
I slowly close my eyes or just stare ahead blankly.
My mind doing its own thing, thinking a million things,
all at the same time.
And at one point of time, I cannot bear it anymore,
I shut down. I let go of my body,
and force shut my brain.
Not a single thought, in or out.
Not a single muscle capable of moving.
Nothing in my mind but a single memory.
A memory which was etched in my mind.
And no matter what I did, I found myself
going back to it when things get difficult.
The memory of you and I, in the bus together.
My head on your shoulder, your hand holding my head,
My hands holding on to your arm,
like you'll disappear the minute I let go.
You held my head, all the while I was sleeping,
making sure I wasn't hurt, every time we crossed a bump.
There are no words in this memory, or any thoughts.
Just you and me, holding on to each other for dear life.
And maybe, subconsciously, that's what keeps me going.
This memory of ours. That even though, you're not here,

You still are, because of this memory.

I feel myself closer to you when I think about it.

Insane, isn't it? How a simple memory,

can be the strength of a person.

19. Ending...

I don't remember when or how I fell asleep,
But I remember the cold air, hitting on my face
from the half open window
with the sun rays falling softly on my face.
I, soon felt a cold hand wrap itself around my sleeping state,
I didn't have to open my eyes to tell that it was you.
You gently pulled me closer to you, stealing all my warmth.
Your cold cheek, touching my warm neck.
Your cold fingers, finding their way to my warm waist.
I moaned into you, finding comfort in our embrace.
My mind then recalled the last two days.
The fort, the sky, the aura, the scene.
And I could only think of one word for it,
mesmerizing. Absolutely mesmerizing.
From the moment we reached there,
to the night we spent under the starry sky,
looking at different constellations.
From the climb up the fort,
to the windy views from the top.
From the cold freezing mornings,
to the warm sunny afternoons,
it was all a bliss, that I had the chance to experience.
And all of it, with you.
Your warm breath on my neck, and
you pulling me in more, brought me back

to the car, on our way home.
I didn't want this to end, not so soon.
But like everything else in life,
every good thing comes to an end eventually.

20. Him

She saw him sitting on the bench from afar,

taking him in, quietly and peacefully.

He was sitting there, leg crossed over the other,

a hardcover book in his hands,

his eyes swiftly shifting across the pages.

His fingers absentmindedly fidgeting with his pen,

his eyes brows scrunched a little,

focused on what's in front of him.

She stared at him, noticing how effortless he was,

like he had absolutely no idea of the effect he had on her.

The wind was blowing tenderly,

through his hair, touching his skin,

making him shiver lightly and pull himself closer.

The wind, along with cold, bringing flowers

from the tree nearby. One lightly landing on

his head, and he, so fluently tucked it in his hair.

And continued reading his book again, so nonchalantly

She chuckled at him, how foolishly charming he was.

She sighed out loud, content and elated.

Making her way to him, she tucked her hair behind her ears.

He looked up when he saw her, "you're late."

She looked at him and just smiled warmly.

"I know", she sat down besides him,

kissing him passionately.

21. Dream?

You walked outside the door,
in all your sleeping glory.
Rubbing your eyes and stifling a yawn,
you walked up to me, mumbled a small good morning.
You sat down beside me in the swing,
and instantly laying down in my lap;
your hands touching my face,
your eyes gazing mine.
I tucked my hair behind my ears,
my fingers making patterns on your chest.
You let go of my face, but held mt hand,
closing your eyes, you made yourself more comfortable.
Tilting my head back, I closed my eyes too,
"10 more minutes", I said. "Yeah, yeah,
10 more minutes of this dream until reality."
you whispered into my hands and fell asleep.

22. Touch

Human touch possesses the ability to calm a person,
to connect with another, to communicate with them,
it excites us with passion and love.
We crave touch, almost
as much as our need to breath.
A gentle caress of fingers,
the soft linger of a hand,
the tender brush of their lips,
the enticing roam of their fingers on your body.
The warm tingling feeling from when their fingers leave,
creates an aching crave of wanting it more.
Then the withdrawal your body goes through,
when it craves their tempting touch, but
doesn't receive it.
The physical pain of not having it,
the mental exhaustion of thinking about it,
the emotional imbalance of wanting it,
the spiritual need of feeling it.
It, their touch, your touch for them.
His touch on my body.

23. Our Time

"I guess, our time wasn't right."
The words ringing in my ear,
your voice echoing again and again.
'Our time' was a period where there was you and me,
when there were two souls, who wanted an 'us'.
'Our time' was when you choose to stay back with me,
instead of going out with your friends;
when it was just you and me and nothing else mattered;
so don't tell me that it isn't our time.
Our time is when we want and when we decide
to stay together, despite all odds.
When it's you and me against the world,
and not you against me and us.
Don't put this karma or life, this is on us.
An 'us' that we let go of because we are scared, terrified even,
scared the other person might walk away,
or wake up one day and all the love is gone.
We are scared of the inevitable heartbreak.
We are scared of something that hasn't even happened yet.
So, all I have to ask you, is a single question,
answer that and I shall never speak to you, of you, ever again.
Answer this, and I will believe that it wasn't our time.
"Do you think ending something so good, so perfect
is the right thing to do just because we are scared of the inevitable?"
Is it not enough to stay in the present and enjoy while we still can?

24. Moments

There are times, moments, fragments of our life,
which hold a permanent place in our mind.
The hippocampus, located in the temporal lobe of our brain
is what holds and nurtures our memories.
Good or bad, sad or happy.
We experience moments of utter happiness,
childish foolishness, intense sorrow,
unexplained agony, unfiltered liberation and more.
And somewhere along these emotions,
we also experience unconditional and passionate love,
for a person, for a thing.
These experiences and emotions, make us who we are,
and they possess the ability to change us,
for better or for worse.
People be it authors or poets or philosophers or a commoner,
all of them have talked, written and spoken
about such experiences and these emotions.
There have been endless poems and words dedicated to
lovers, partners, enemies, families, admirers and others.
Is this going to be one such poem on love, you ask?
Yes, it is, it ought to be. You see,
for a person who considers themselves to be a romantic,
it is inevitable for them to write about love,
at least once in their lifetime. It is bound for their soul,
to crave, need, breathe and experience love.

Because, if not, then how will they spend the rest of lives,

fervently in love with a person, trying to

make them eternal with their words.

We need love and touch, almost

as much as, we need air to breathe. To survive.

These memories make their way in our minds,

in a way that even on our death beds,

we would know exactly how it felt,

to be with the person we love.

We remember the exact moment,

love takes over us and we lose all our defense.

We remember the fireworks and butterflies,

in our stomach, in our entire bodies

when we first touched them, a soft graze of the fingers.

A touch, so gentle, so exhilarating that it lights up our body.

For us, it's how perfectly our fingers fit with theirs,

that sends our body into euphoria.

Like a match made in hell, our story begins from that moment.

From a moment of euphoria, from a moment of tenderness.

A moment, we take to our death beds, we take to our graves.

A moment, where we give ourselves to that one person,

who makes us feel unconditionally loved.

25. Perfect Day

It was around 6 in the evening,
and I was in your arms, under the blanket.
Our warm bodies entangled with each other,
our skin pressing against and touching together.

We had spent the day together,
just being in each others presence.
There were conversations, silences and gazing,
there was touching of the skin and gentle collide of the lips.

The sky was orange with the setting sun,
the birds were chirping their way home.
The flute in the background tied everything together,
the soft melody filling in the space of words.

that was the end of a perfect day,
a day that will come with me to my grave.

26. That Moment

We were born as humans, and
one good thing about being a human,
is that as you get on with your life,
you make memories, both good and bad ones.
The more you live, the more memories you create,
The more memories you create, the more your mind remembers,
The more you remember, the more you tend to go back to that
memory,
The more you go back, the more you relive those emotions and
feelings of that memory.
But with time, you heal, your soul grows
and your brain, slowly begins to forget the bad memories.
As time goes by, you barely remember the reason of that fight,
or the words that were said in anger.
And all you're left with, is a big pile of
happy, blissful memories.
These are the memories you remember clearly,
you remember the exact events, the feelings,
the words, as if it was just yesterday.
You remember how you walked along
the 'Non-fiction' aisle with your lover,
you remember sneaking kisses,
when the people weren't looking.
You remember feeling giddy and excited,
to be in that place with them.

You remember the small details of
hands touching and eyes gazing,
You remember the details and those moments,
because, in that moment you felt happy,
you were happy and safe in their arms.
Without a care for the future, you wanted
time to stop in that moment,
so you would never have to leave them.
And after all that time, when you think
back to that same memory, you still wish
for time to take you back to that day.
you still wish for time to stop,
where you were happy and content,
in a small bookstore, holding the hands of your lover.

27. Their Prescence

One thing about life, is that
no matter how much you plan,
things tend to go off the road.
No matter how detailed your itinerary is,
there will come a time when life takes on its own.
You might have decided what you want for lunch,
but, life might have some other lunch plans for you.
So, you never know, what would happen next;
you never know if you'll make it back home
or if you'll see your favorite person again.
And by the time you realize that, that
was the last time you'd see them,
a cloud forms over you.
A cloud of sadness, grief, shock and regret...
your heart sinks to the bottom of the ocean,
your mind stops functioning properly,
your hands quiver a little bit,
your legs seem to have forgotten how to walk.
Despite all of that, you get up the next day,
with your body physically in pain,
your head as heavy as a mountain,
your eyes swollen like a bee sting,
you get up and try to get on with your life.
As you get on with your life, you come across
things that remind you of them.

A small trinket around the house,
a favorite book, or something they gave you.
When that happens, your body stops for a few seconds,
you hear your heart beat loudly in your ear,
your body perspires a little bit, until
you remember that they're not here, and
this is just their memory.
You relive the moment you spent with them,
thinking back to every single day or time
you were with them and what all you did.
At times, when you're lost in thought about them
you feel their touch on your skin,
or hear their faint voice in the back of your head,
you subconsciously choose their favorite things,
and suddenly get the urge to tell them your best moments of the day,
until you realize, again, that they are not here.
It happens more times then you can control,
because they are there in your soul,
they became a part of your soul
when you had them, and now
when they aren't here, you don't know what to do.
I don't know what to do, because you aren't here with me.
I struggle each day, thinking 'just get through today and you'll be
okay'
until tomorrow comes and I repeat the same thing.
But in all honesty, all I wish for, is to go back
to the time with you. The time when you were with me.
All I wish for is to, hold your hand one last time,
all I wish for is to kiss your lips,

embrace you fully in my arms,
look at you a little while longer,
and to say that I love you,
and that I wish that things were better.
All I wish for is to be with you, one last time
and I promise to make that time last forever,
so that you never have to leave.
But sadly, you're only in my memory now,
a huge part of memory that I shall never forget.

28. If I Knew

If I knew that we would last only for a while,
I would have hugged you more,
I would have given you more forehead kisses.
I would have danced with you more.

If I knew that would be the last time I saw you,
I would have held you a little longer,
I would have cuddled with you more.
I would have stayed with you for longer.

If I knew our time would last only for a while,
I wouldn't have ever fought with you.
I wouldn't have said anything to hurt you.
I would have spent more time,
being with you, day and night.

If I knew our time would only last for a while,
I would have let you be the little spoon,
I would have showered you with all the love I had in me.
I would have spent more time talking to you,
listening to you about your day and your life.

If I knew...that our time would only last for while,
I would have never let you go...ever.

29. A Lover's Life

Ever since time immemorial,
poets were known for creating magic with their words.
Their skill was to blend fantasy with reality,
and let the reader dissolve into it.
And every poet, at least once in their lives,
has written about their beloved person.
We may write about hundreds of other things,
but there's always a single poem, a single person,
who always reflects in our work.
We get enchanted by that one person,
so hypnotized and lost, that we make them ours.
We make them ours, from our mind, soul and body.
Every breath we take, every word that leaves our mouth,
is somehow bound by that person, our person.
So, we decidedly write a poem for them,
about them, about our thoughts of them.
we let the words from our minds,
flow till the tip of our pens,
to that huge blank white sheet,
which gets filled with love, lust and emotion
by the time we've come to an end.
We let that paper be our canvas,
and fill it with moments we've experienced with our beloved,
or we fill it with the moments we dream about experiencing with
them.

We write about the dreams we've had,

the fantasy we get lost into--

when they're not with us,

We write about the moments they were with us,

the moments our skin touched and the eyes met.

Poets don't let a thought go unheard,

our minds scream when we ignore what they say,

and the easiest way we know on how to quiet our minds,

is to pen what it says. So, we pen them down.

Every reality we saw, every dream we dreamed, we write it all down.

And eventually, as we write,

we let ourselves dissolve into it.

30. Your Relationship

There are some relationships in our life,
that either make us or break us.
And among those few relationships,
There's that one particular relationship,
Which breaks us, no matter how much we try to make it.
It breaks us to a point where we shatter,
our heart breaks into a million pieces,
like shards of glass.
We break to a point, where it seems
difficult to gather back up.
But the thing about that relationship is,
that they actually make us, instead of breaking us.
It's the loss of that relationship, that breaks us,
but it's only for a while,
until our mind, body and soul
all emote the tornado of feelings we feel.
We feel broken and helpless for ourselves,
because our heart cannot bear the loss,
our mind cannot comprehend what happened,
our soul cannot tell what's missing.
So, we feel as if that that's it,
this is the end. From this point onward,
we would never be the same. But,
there comes a turning point,
a moment of realization, the moment we snap back

to reality. It all becomes clear.
That our relationship, whose loss we mourned,
taught us and changed us for better.
Changed how we look at things,
taught us lessons no one else did.
And this realization dawns upon us,
while we're doing something ordinary,
like writing something, or drinking water
or hearing a song or cleaning your desk.
The realization is so subtle and subconscious,
that you almost miss it for a fleeting thought.
But it comes back to you, when you realize,
you've arranged things in a manner they liked,
or you write certain words differently as they taught you.
The change becomes your pattern,
a part of who you are, engulfs you as a whole,
to a point, where it doesn't bother you,
it doesn't make you feel broken,
or your heart doesn't ache when you think about them.
Instead, you smile, a very faint almost content smile,
thinking about them, about your memories with them.
You bask is the happiness of when you were with them.
You bask in the relationship that made you.

31. Take me

There was a cup of coffee on the table,
black with bubbles at the side.
I could see my reflection in it,
wild hair, bright eyes, flushed face.
I think I stared too much at my reflection,
at that cup of black coffee, because
when I looked up, you were there.
You were sitting across the table from me,
smiling like a Cheshire cat.
You were wearing a black full sleeves t-shirt,
with your favourite dark denim and white Converse.
I felt a warm faded feeling in my chest.
The table was now filled with plates of food,
and empty cups of coffee.
I could feel myself yapping away,
like an excited little puppy,
telling you every single detail,
every single insecurity I ever had,
every addiction, every strength,
every weakness and vulnerability.
I remember telling you everything,
breathing and taking you in,
your scent, your skin, your touch.
Letting you become a part of me,
every breath, every blink, every sigh.

There was an empty white plate,
in the center of our table.
And in the middle of it,
was a bloody beating heart, my heart.
I slowly slid the plate towards you,
giving you my heart, my soul, my mind.
Letting you take me away,
from this anarchic world.
In a blink of an eye, I was back here.
Back to the table, sitting alone,
with a cup of black coffee and a flushed face.
As I took a sip from the cup,
you called out my name,
your beautiful voice ringing in my ears.
We smiled widely at each other,
you took my hand in yours,
and it was as if, a small piece of me
had been found.
Like, I could finally breathe again.
Like, my world was finally at peace again.

32. Safe Space

She quickly ran up the stairs,

huffing and puffing, she just ran

opening the door to her room,

she quickly twisted the lock key,

securing the door, she stumbled towards

her cupboard, sliding the doors open,

haphazardly pulling out clothes and boxes,

making a space big enough for her.

Without looking back at the mess she made,

she made herself so small, so minute,

almost disappearing in the space she cleared.

She slid the doors close, entirely.

She could hear her heart thumping in her ears,

her hands shaking, body trembling.

She sighed, a deep long sigh,

putting her head back, relaxing her body,

closing her eyes, she took deep breaths.

She was safe, no one could harm her,

no one could reach for her, touch her,

The cupboard was her safe space.

She could still hear the faint shouting,

Two, maybe three voices, arguing, yelling.

There was a loud rumble and she froze,

the incessant rumbling put her into panic,

her hands frantically looking for something,

something to hold onto, something to use as a weapon.
But then the rumbling stopped, suddenly
it was quiet, eerily quiet.
She immediately knew, he had left,
he had gone, furiously out the door.
Her vision became weak, black spots appeared
she had held in her breath, without realizing,
she wasn't breathing, out of fear.
She exhaled, almost losing consciousness
she relaxed her hands, her head, her body
all of which had frozen in shock.
She let her body sink more into the cupboard,
letting the darkness take over.
She let her eyes close and curled up her body,
she breathed a sigh of relief, for she knew
that she was now out of danger,
she was safe, and nothing in the world
could get to her. She was safe, in these wooden walls
surrounded by darkness, her old friend.

33. Pink Fabric

She unpacked her bag
putting everything back in its place
'do not touch' read the tag
hanging with a tied lace

In the midst of it all,
fell a pink napkin in her hand
she caught it's gentle fall
remembering the incident unplanned

She touched the fabric
felt it between her fingers
she felt emphatic,
But it bothered her trigger

She held it against her nose
a deep inhale of the smell
she lost balance, curling her toes
as if she had been put under a spell

His smell was lingering on the fabric
and memories were making her ecstatic
she closed her to eyes to relish the moment
but somewhere between was also atonement

She held it in her fingers tight,
for she knew she wouldn't do anything tonight
she climbed into bed in the dark
drowning in moments of their spark.

34. Petals Painted Pale

You know, that funny feeling you get
when you're on a roller coaster
and it goes down, that's the feeling
I felt before it all went black.
The funny, nauseous sinking feeling
before the world around me became
distorted and I faded into nothingness.
I was falling down, but the world was slow
I expected a tragic fall, but instead
was greeted with a soft landing
on a bed of green moist grass.
Laying on the ground, in my faded glory
I felt weightless, without a single worry
my thoughts never been so crystal,
my body never felt so free.
A shadow cast over my feet,
A figure I could never forget,
A person, imprinted on my soul,
The shadow moved, and the person
came into view, in his hands was a
beautifully wrapped bouquet, a skill
that I was a master of.
A colourful canvas of yellow, white, pink
and purple chrysanthemums in his hand.
I closed my eyes and inhaled their smell,

when I opened them back, I was away
from myself and from him, 5 feet away
He fell on his knees, the bouquet
falling to the ground, near my feet
He placed them by my face,
my pale, ghostly, lifeless face.
He didn't say a word, not a single sound
he just sat there, for hours on end
holding a very cold hand, in his warm ones.
I walked towards myself, the grass soft
and warm under my bare feet,
I made myself comfortable,
on the opposite side of him.
Reaching out, I felt the petals of the flowers
I pulled out a purple one, and tucked it
on my ear, letting it adorn my pale face
We sat there in silence, you looking at me
me looking at you and the flowers your brought me,
wondering how I would have squealed in excitement,
had I received then a day before,
when I wasn't laying pale, on the cold grass
wondering, how it never occurred to you,
that I liked getting flowers, especially
Chrysanthemums, they were my favorites,
thinking about how you knew about them,
as you'd never asked me about my favourite flower.
It's cruel, how a person fades away from this world
hoping, craving, aching for something as frivolous
as getting flowers, or receiving a small card.

It's cruel how the world works like that,
where it fills the person left behind, with
such sorrow and heavy regret, it leaves them
with extreme guilt for the rest of eternity
for not being the person they should have been
for not acknowledging that faded soul.
And then, they're left with no option
but to bring their dead cold grave flowers,
and then watching those flowers die
because the other person,
who would have taken care of them,
isn't here. Its romance disguised in cruelty.
A dying, decaying romance.

35. Worlds Apart

The night was dark, the room dimly lit
the windows were open, the curtains stagnant
the air was chilly, the atmosphere heavy
the song playing the background, the room silent

I was laying on the bed, you were sitting up
your head was on one side, mine was on the other
my hand was lingering in between, yours was too
you were lost in thought, I was lost in you

our eyes were closed, thinking about how things were
our minds telepathic, fingers finding their to each other
our eyes getting teary, hands squeezing strongly
our hearts beating loudly, filling the silence

I open my eyes to look at you,
you move towards me,
our bodies meet and embrace each other
our worlds, broken separately
but complete together.

36. Fated Lovers

We were pieces of puzzles, two different puzzles,
a round and a square, a rectangle and a square.

We were opposites in the domains of the world;
an emotional and a practical person,
an introvert and an extrovert, creating an ambivert,
a caring soul with a coconut shell.

Our puzzles were never meant to mingle,
but fate seemed to be in a cheerful mood.
a mood, that brought light to darkness,
that brought black and white to color.

Two pieces of different puzzle, you and I
brought together by the choice of fate.

37. The Sound Of Home

People say "home" is a feeling,
It is not four walls of concrete that provide you with shelter,
But it is the feeling of safety when you hug the person you love.
I don't disagree, you are home to me.
There is safety in your arms.
But, you are the safety that I feel,
when I drive under a bridge in a thunder strom.
You are the safety that I feel when,
the sound of the raging rain crashing on the hood of my car stops.
When the constant fear of something bad happening,
fades away, even if it for a few seconds;
there is safety and love in that momentary silence,
where I know that I will come back home.
Home, the comfort of your arms around me.

38. Mine, Yours, Ours.

I open my eyes, you are there
I open my eyes and my heart flutters
it flutters at your mesmerizing sight,
I open my eyes...to you.

I reminisce in an old memory,
the lyrics to our song,
I sing the song to you,
falling for you...again.

I see a pond, and I stop there
the familiar pond being ours
ours, because you took me there
I see a pond and I drown in you.

I open the book, a way to your heart
the title, your name
your name, written by yours truly
I open the book, a love story of ours.

When I wrote each of my poems, I didn't know that it will lead to this day. I decided to publish my poems in 2020, but it took me two years to finally do it. Two years of contemplation and nervousness about whether or not this was a good idea or not, whether or not my book will be appreciated or acknowledged. Keeping all my anxiety aside, here I stand, open and vulnerable in front of a stranger, hoping to provide and seek comfort in the likeliness of our lives.